"I pray my daughter has the [...] made her, and Shannon Evans [...] and beautifully crafted words [...] deep wisdom of Christian trad[...] [...]nds us that—even if we cannot protect our daughters from the hard choices ahead or the grief that is sure to come—we can do what mothers have always done and pray them through it."

—**Beth Allison Barr**, professor, Baylor University; bestselling author of *The Making of Biblical Womanhood*

"Shannon Evans has written a beautiful book of feminist prayers that are full of care, authenticity, and nuance—clear and gentle guidance for parents and children alike. The words and images in these pages will be a balm for many, reminding us that Sacred Mystery is always beckoning us home."

—**Kaitlin B. Curtice**, bestselling author of *Native* and *Living Resistance*

"*Feminist Prayers for My Daughter* is like coming into a harbor of hope. I have longed for a creative, robust voice like that of Shannon Evans. The prayers in this book are a treasure. Evans's approach to divinity as lived in daily life will inspire and encourage women, both young and old, to pray and live as their freest, truest, and wisest selves."

—**Joyce Rupp**, author of *Prayers to Sophia* and *The Star in My Heart*

"So much of mothering a daughter is wordless: an embodied longing for a world in which she is fully connected to herself and others, a heartache knowing she will face pain, an uncontainable awe at the delight of who she is becoming, a bow of the head to Mother God to show us both the way. Evans offers us words where there often aren't any. She shows us how and what to pray for our daughters, because when our daughters are treasured, free to live their lives fully, it is better for us all."

—**Hillary L. McBride**, psychologist, author, speaker, and podcaster

"The words in *Feminist Prayers for My Daughter* are rooted in the sacred and divine. Exquisitely woven, they took me through my own journey as daughter, mother, woman, and healer. May we all read these words to remind us of our inherent worth and beauty, and may they nourish the flames of the feminine rising. This book is revolutionary for these times. I cannot recommend it enough."

—**Asha Frost**, Indigenous healer; bestselling author of *You Are the Medicine*

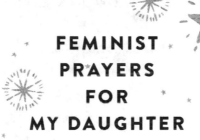

FEMINIST PRAYERS FOR MY DAUGHTER

FEMINIST PRAYERS FOR MY DAUGHTER

POWERFUL PETITIONS
FOR EVERY STAGE OF HER LIFE

SHANNON K. EVANS

 **Brazos**Press

a division of Baker Publishing Group
Grand Rapids, Michigan

© 2023 by Shannon K. Evans

Published by Brazos Press
a division of Baker Publishing Group
Grand Rapids, Michigan
www.brazospress.com

Printed in the United States of America

Library of Congress Cataloging-in-Publication Data
Names: Evans, Shannon K., 1978– author.
Title: Feminist prayers for my daughter : powerful petitions for every stage of her life / Shannon K. Evans.
Description: Grand Rapids, Michigan : Brazos Press, a division of Baker Publishing Group, [2023]
Identifiers: LCCN 2022026448 | ISBN 9781587435492 (paperback) | ISBN 9781587436000 (casebound) | ISBN 9781493440368 (pdf) | ISBN 9781493440351 (ebook)
Subjects: LCSH: Mothers—Prayers and devotions. | Daughters—Prayers and devotions. | Women—Prayers and devotions.
Classification: LCC BV4847 .E93 2023 | DDC 242/.6431—dc23/eng/20220713
LC record available at https://lccn.loc.gov/2022026448

The author is represented by WordServe Literary Group, www.wordserveliterary.com.

Illustrations © Rosanna Tasker / IllustrationX, IllustrationX.com

23 24 25 26 27 28 29   7 6 5 4 3 2 1

For my parents,
who have prayed some iteration of
these prayers every day of my life

And, of course,
for Thea Moon

CONTENTS

EQUALITY

MILESTONES

PREFACE

My daughter was not exactly "planned." Quite the opposite really. The surprise positive pregnancy test came just a few weeks before my fourth son turned one. We weren't sure there would be any more babies after him, and certainly not for a few years, but I couldn't find a trace of anxiety inside myself. I just knew, right from the beginning, that this was my daughter.

Perhaps the sense of deep knowing came because at that time I was in a reckoning with my faith tradition over the ways God is masculinized at the expense of the feminine. I was angry that God can be called he and not she. I was exhausted by the all-male hierarchy within Catholicism, the church tradition I belong to. I was adamant that Christians needed to be disentangling ourselves from racism, homophobia, colonization, and xenophobia, and I believed that female leadership would move that work forward. I was longing to relate to God as mother, not just father, but was unsure whether that would ever feel comfortable.

Then, mere days after finding out about the pregnancy, a book I had painstakingly written was pulled straight off the printer by a bishop who deemed me too dangerous to represent the prominent women's ministry publishing the book. There is no overemphasizing the deep shift that occurred in me after this, and it had more than a little to do with the fact that I was carrying in my womb what I knew to be a little girl. She gave me something to fight for—some*one* to fight for. In the loneliest hours of my faith, when I've been ready to light a match to the whole thing, the life of my daughter has made me stubborn and brave. I cannot walk away from a God who gave her to me in my time of need.

Instead, I have accepted the invitation to reimagine this God I once thought I had pegged: the God who is neither male nor female yet both masculine and feminine; the God who shapeshifts into the symbol or metaphor we need at any given moment; the God who transcends language but still invites its use; the God whom some mystics called Mother, and others, Lover. As I wrestle with my own way of being with a God who is endlessly more mysterious than I once believed God to be, I feel a sense of awe at the idea of my daughter one day doing the same. It's true that this book came from my own need for more liberated ideas about God, but it also came from the longing for my daughter to know God—and in coming to know God to better know herself—in this way much sooner than I did.

The word "feminist" in the title of this book is quite literal in its definition of simply believing that women are inherently equal to men. But it is important to me to acknowledge the harm that has come upon the BIPOC, LGBTQ, and impoverished

communities from the activism of white feminist political movements that has left them behind. I bow with gratitude to woman-
ist theologians in particular who have been leading voices in this
social critique. I hope and pray that women of all backgrounds
can find themselves and their daughters in the pages of this book.

I have carefully chosen the names by which I address God
in these prayers. Some are derived from the Bible. Others are
metaphors crafted by my prayerful imagination. No single name
could ever be expansive enough for the one whom we call God,
but I like to think that if we use as many as we can conceive of,
we might begin to scratch the surface of the great I Am.

This book is for mothers, yes, but it is also for fathers, grand-
parents, godparents, aunts and uncles, cousins, stepparents, sisters, foster parents, coaches, mentors, pastors, chaplains, teachers,
and family friends. It is, perhaps most of all, for women who are
re-mothering themselves. It is for the churched and the "nones,"
the devout and the doubters, those who lead congregations and
those who never step foot in a house of worship. It is for those
who want to see a healthier, safer, more equitable world for our
girls. It is for all who are determined to clear the brush, machete
in one arm and daughter in the other, until there is a path for
her where once there was none.

RELATIONSHIPS

for supportive female friendships

Devoted Companion,

At this and every stage of my daughter's life,
bring her female friends who will be faithful and true.

Protect their hearts from jealousy and insecurity,
betrayal and comparison.
May they lift one another up,
reveling in each other's successes as though they were their own
(seeing that, in fact, they are).
May they share secrets and share clothes,
share books and share dreams.
May they delight in each other's individuality
and appreciate their differences.
May their friendship propel each girl to become more fully herself.

There will be those who will use them and lose them,
those who will grow tired of them,

those who will be threatened by them,
but this I pray:
may my daughter and her girlfriends find all they need by linking
arms together.

Amen.

for daughterhood

O Tender Parent,

In every stage of my daughter's life, what she has needed from me as a parent has changed, and I understand that our relationship will continue to shift and morph. Help her to express what she needs from me as she grows. Help me to be intuitive and responsive to her needs.

As a daughter, may unconditional love be the foundation upon which she stands. May she always feel supported and embraced by her family. May our belief in and delight of her be the most fundamental truths she knows.

When the time comes for her to seek identity outside of her family, help me affirm and support that need. When she is ready to become a woman, let it be a transition made with grace. Help me honor her choices. Help me appreciate our differences. Help me trust her—and trust you with her.

I pray that my love could be the bedrock of my daughter's life, on which she builds an identity and experience of her own. May I never cling so tightly that she can't be free. May I always be a safe place for her to choose to return.

Amen.

for handling peer pressure

O Everpresent Strength,

In these adolescent days, as my daughter seeks to find out who she is, she will look to her peers to help her decide. Grant her wisdom in choosing who she surrounds herself with, knowing that they will hold up a mirror for her own reflection.

When the opinions of others carry her away,
ground her in experiential self-knowing.

When she feels the need to dress like other girls,
show her how to make the styles her own.

When she wishes to simply blend into the crowd,
bring her back to the unique magic of her particular flame.

When she is tempted to limit what she eats,
remind her that her body is worthy of nourishment.

When her peers are experimenting with substance abuse, give her clarity of mind and spirit.

When she feels the expectation of crossing her own boundaries, be her ever-present strength.

May my daughter have a vision of the woman she is to become, and may no one convince her it is not enough.

Amen.

for her broken heart

O Source of All Comfort,

The heart is a fragile thing, and my daughter's is now broken.

She put her hope in love, and it seems to have failed her.
She made herself vulnerable and now bears the weight of regret.
Having given of herself fully and freely, she wonders if she will
ever feel whole again.

There are wounds so deep even I cannot mend them. I feel help-
less against her pain.

So come, Soothing Mother, perfect in comfort, and speak to my
daughter your deep and ancient truths.

Stroke her hair and tuck her in and sing over her of the worthiness
of love. How it wounds us. How it can also repair us. And how
both make us more beautiful than we once could see.

Amen.

for commitment

O Mystical Union,

My daughter has chosen partnership in _____ (choose the situation that applies: romance, engagement, community, vocation, etc.). She is ready to devote herself faithfully and sacrificially to the good of more than just herself.

For this commitment she is making, I pray:

May she find joy in the journey she has chosen;
give her laughter every day.

May she practice safe listening;
guide her in the ways of receptivity without judgment.

May she uphold healthy boundaries for herself;
help her see that this, too, is generosity.

May she be stubborn in hope;
teach her to fight for it, come what may.

In all the ways that this commitment will unfold as she plans, and for all the many more ways that it won't, may my daughter be fully present at every turn, ready to grow and expand and be changed for the better.

Amen.

for consensual sex

O God of Self-Belonging,

My daughter's body is a temple.
May all who seek to enter tremble at such holy ground.

In a world where confusion about sex abounds, may one thing
be simple:
her body belongs only to her.
Her sacred, glorious, wonder-full body belongs,
ever and always, only to her.

She owes a high school classmate nothing.
She owes a middle-aged husband nothing.

May her yes mean yes
and her no mean no.

Put the fear of God in anyone who would think otherwise.

Amen.

for becoming a mother

O First Mother,

Magic has erupted.
My daughter is now a mother.

Broken open by wonder, I lift her to the communion of saints, to each and every mother who has gone before her, and to you, First Mother. You have labored and birthed and fed and nourished and washed and tended from the dawn of time.

I pray, bless this new mother.
Bless this wide-eyed one who is both elated and terrified, awed and pained.
Bless her with your ancient name.
Bless her with her own.
Bless her with an expanded capacity to hold the new cosmos that has burst forth within her heart.

Bless her with the belief, deep into her bones, that she can do this.

Amen.

for singleness

O Source of Abundant Wholeness,

In you we find ourselves whole.
In you there is only fruitfulness.
In you we lack nothing.

My daughter lacks nothing, least of all a "better half." She is not a half, but a whole; not a woman in waiting, but a woman fully alive and passionate.

When those around her are marrying, let her rejoice for them, knowing her life is equally as full of love.

When her friends and peers begin their families, let her celebrate mightily, knowing she is a vital part of the great human family.

When loneliness sets in, let her remember how to revel in her own fascinating company.

May those around her choose their words carefully: not fixating on her romantic status but on her impact on the world, not seeing something missing but seeing something abundantly present.

May she and all who know her see a woman whose very existence is a fountain of love and fruitfulness.

Amen.

for rewilding motherhood

O Untamed One,

The years of sacrifice have worn down my daughter. She delights in her children but wonders at how she became so docile, so bone-tired. She feels she barely knows herself anymore and dreams of a far-off day when her life will be hers again.

Rewild her.

Ignite a spark in her that lets her dare to believe there is more than this. Pique a curiosity in her that wonders what it means to be made in the image of an untamed God. Introduce her to the organic matter in her soul and leave her to play there.

Give her the courage to forge the walls of her own interior castle and be enamored by what she finds. May it make her feel wild, alive, raw, inspired. May she find herself waking up.

Open her eyes to the invitation you have extended to her right here in the life she is living now. Give her a contemplative spirit that can find wonder and mystery in all things: the minutiae of everyday life, the constant needs of her children, and especially within herself.

In all the places of her soul that have been pushed aside for the sake of motherhood, may the buds of self-reclamation begin to sprout. May she discover the wild wonder within.

Amen.

for a shame-free sexual ethic

O Marvelous Liberator,

To you whose rapture sustains the world, at whose right hand are pleasures forevermore, this is my prayer.

Let my daughter know the innocence of shame-free sex.
Let her delight unapologetically in her body and in the body of her lover.
Let her express herself as a creature designed for physical abundance and joy.
Let her have really great sex.

Protect my daughter from voices that would try to make her ashamed.
Protect her from those who would downplay the importance of her pleasure.
Protect her from unequal intimacy.
Protect her from partners who would use coercion.

Protect her, O Marvelous Liberator, from a sexuality that is not whole.

May my daughter possess an integrated sexuality that brings her back to herself; a sexuality that makes her feel fully alive and inspired; a sexuality that supports her voice, agency, and well-being. May she be like Eve: naked and unashamed.

Amen.

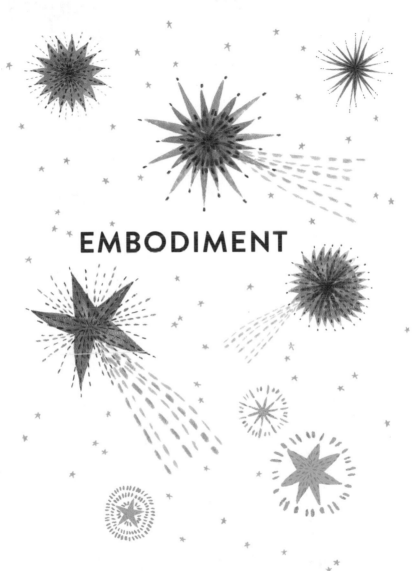

EMBODIMENT

for body acceptance

O Embodied Spirit,

You who have your being in trees and mole rats and pebbles and human flesh, let my daughter notice you when her toes bury in sand, when there is garden dirt deep in her nail beds, when the light hits the curve of her hip just so.

Let her believe this is beauty. And on the days when she doesn't quite believe it, let her at least concede that it's pretty good anyway.

I know she is watching me watch myself. She listens as I speak to myself. May it be the joy and wonder of being alive that she sees and hears. May it be the pleasure of having a body, at all phases and stages, that my daughter learns. May she see me enjoy myself living this one stunner of a life.

May she see me living in my body—no matter what others say about it—feeling

strong,
sexy,
beautiful,
nurturing,
soft,
welcoming,
embracing,
supportive,
celebratory,
awake.

May I fill us both with so many true words that there is no room left for the untrue ones.

Amen.

for seeing color

O First Artist,

You have delighted in the creation of skin color.
You have created a kaleidoscope of humanity.

When my daughter first notices the skin of her neighbor,
may the revelation bring a celebration of diversity.

When she asks questions about other ethnicities,
may her curiosity lead to appreciation.

When she learns about racism's potent history,
may it stir within her courage and empathy.

When I am the one she looks to for answers,
give me wisdom, clarity, and honesty.

When another suggests it is best to be colorblind,
bring to her mind the beauty of a tapestry.

May she reject the idolization of colorblindness.
May she *see* color.

And in seeing color, may she see each person for who they are.

Amen.

for when gender boxes are too small

O Nonbinary Spirit,

You surpass every construct of gender that we have understood or imagined. You are at once nothing and everything the human mind can comprehend. And in this blessed way, you have chosen to make your mystery known through my daughter.

When she suffers from the ways her body does not reflect her soul, comfort and affirm her. May she believe you see her, in all her complexities, exactly for who she is.

When she questions herself, be near her. Give her the grace to wrestle with you. Give her the security of knowing you aren't going anywhere.

When she buckles under insecurity, raise her up, head held high. Redirect her to the compass you have placed deep within her.

When she chooses freedom, send those who will celebrate with her. Surround her with those who can look into her eyes and name her beloved. I pray that we, her family, may always be first among those.

And when she feels discounted from and left out of religious circles, give her greater clarity of the particular way she embodies the transcendent, genderless God of extravagant love.

Amen.

for disabilities

O Crown Bestower,

My daughter does not possess the same abilities that others do. In some ways, her life may be harder. Such things scare me, if I'm honest, and the unknown future scares me most.

And yet I look at this girl and I see a queen. You have placed a crown on her head and a mantle on her spirit. She has fight in her. She has grit. She has great dignity. May she always know who she is; may she always carry her crown with poise.

My daughter will make her mark on the world in her own way and in her own time. May every dream of the universe for this child of mine be fulfilled, no matter how many times she hears the words "can't" or "won't." Spare me from being the one to utter such words in her ear. Spare all who love her from attempting to hold her back out of our own fear.

May her differing abilities only make her more creative and resourceful. May my daughter's struggles one day become her glory.

Amen.

for aging

O Mother Time,

We are told that aging is a curse.
On the contrary, aging is the greatest of your gifts, for it is the gift of more time.
Let my daughter embrace her aging body in appreciation for the boundless love and wisdom that are stored therein.

Let my daughter age, O Mother Time.
Let her face wrinkle,
let there be lines around her lips,
let her hands boast liver spots,
let gravity pull on her stomach,
let her breasts sag,
let my daughter's hair go gray and wiry,
let her ankles complain of varicose veins,
let her moles grow unseemly hairs.

Let my daughter age
and rejoice in her aging,
for it is only in aging that she lives.

Amen.

for celebrating breasts

O Breasted God,

You who allow our heads to rest on your heavenly bosom, instill in my daughter a sense of delight in her own breasts. May they make her proud and not ashamed; may she be ever disinclined to compare or criticize the unique shape and size of her beautiful body.

I pray that my daughter would hold her head high from her place in the lineage of our family's women, bonding and giggling with her female relatives over the landscapes of our figures.

May she know her place among women who nurture,
women who nurse,
women who nourish,
women who bring beauty when they walk into a room.

May the softness of her curves, big or small, remind her of the legacy from which she comes.

Amen.

for getting her hands dirty

O You Who Dwell in Dirt and Worms,

My daughter comes from the earth, and to the earth she will return.
May she ever find a home in the dirt.

My daughter plants seeds and harvests supper.
May she know the land will always give her what she needs.

My daughter feeds the chickens in the evenings and gathers eggs
in the morning.
May she cultivate relationships of reciprocity with all living things.

My daughter has lost and buried beloved birds and bunnies and
goldfish in this circle of life.
May she remember their deaths the way she remembers their
lives.

My daughter plants wildflowers for the sheer beauty of the
blooms.

May she always count their beauty as a valid end in itself.

My daughter has been taught by the earth how to love and how to care.
May she live with the intention of returning the favor.

Amen.

for dynamic movement

O Rushing Wind,

We experience you in movements, both within us and around us. You are love in constant motion. Reveal to my daughter the delights of feeling her body move. Reveal to her the ways she can come to know herself through physical movement; reveal the ways it opens her up to authentically know you.

Guide her to the kind of physical movement that will best stir her soul:
not the movement her peers are doing,
not the movement that wins social accolades,
not the movement that earns a college scholarship,
not the movement most hidden from public sight.

Guide her to the movement that her body craves, the movement her body thrives on, the movement her body needs to encounter you in her own particular way.

Amen.

for pregnancy

O Womb of the World,

New life grows inside my daughter, and we are on our knees with awe.

As the weeks tick by and my daughter's body grows and adjusts to contain this kind of love, give her patience with the process. Give her patience with herself. Teach her to bear discomfort and suffering for the sake of another.

May health and safety encircle the two of them; may they be protected from all distress.

Surround my daughter with the care and support of ones who believe in her and in the ability of her womanhood.

In the places she feels afraid, give her courage.
In the places she feels unequipped, give her reassurance.
In the places she feels overwhelmed, give her peace.

When she is most weary, O Womb of the World, fill her with wonder: the wonder of having created something out of nothing. May she stand in worship at the mystery of the ages: the mystery of love's generativity.

Amen.

for miscarriage and infant loss

O Grief Carrier,

My daughter's baby is with you now, and it feels as though nothing could ever be right in the world again.
Our hearts are broken.
My daughter weeps.
Her body mourns.

We do not understand. We do not understand. We do not understand.

We are so angry.

So desperately sad.

And yet, where else can we go? You have the words of eternal life.

Hold my daughter.
Carry her grief.

Contain her longing.
Let her tears pool up in your bosom.
Allow her to yell and rail against you.
Stretch out your arms when she wears herself out.

My daughter's body carried a miracle.
Now it is asked to see that miracle to the other side.
As grief rolls through her body, may it be a love song to the one she could not keep.

Amen.

SPIRITUALITY

for an inner compass

O North Star,

When you wove together my daughter's innermost being,
you stitched a compass deep within,
so she would always know where to find you.

Remind her now that, by her very design, she can never lose you.
For you are in her and she is in you;
all she must do is still herself and listen.

Some will say she cannot be trusted to find your star.
They will insist she needs their rules,
their boundaries, and their interpretations.

When they come for my daughter, O Star of the Night,
stir within her the memories of each and every time she
sought you
and found you for herself.

Let her not be fooled, either, by those who will discourage
her seeking
by denying you will ever be found.
Make her sharp and astute;
strengthen within her the muscles of instinct and trust.

Make her a student of the compass within,
so that wherever she travels, she walks toward you—
and in doing so, she walks toward her truest self.

Amen.

for a lost sheep

O Loving Shepherdess,

The day will come when my innocent baby will grow curious and reckless beneath the light of the moon, when she will try to find herself by losing herself—and her losing herself will break my heart.

On that day, I beg you, protect my daughter.
Show her the path of life: the narrow way that winds through her limbs, gut, and heart.
Reveal to her who she is and what she wants.
Reveal to her the unmet needs behind foolish actions.

Give me the courage to let my daughter wander, to promise her that she can never lose me, or my love, or the light on my front porch.

When she gets lost, as little sheep do, fill me with gentleness and understanding. Fill me with mercy. And carry my daughter in the crook of your great cosmic arm until she can once more find her way back home.

Amen.

for sacred listening

O Still, Small Voice,

I am comforted in knowing that my daughter has access to
you at any time or in any place.
Teach her, I pray, how to know where to find you deep within
herself.
Teach her what you sound like.
Teach her the ways of sacred listening.

When she must make a decision, may she listen for your
voice.
When she feels alone, may she listen for your presence.
When she needs wisdom, may she listen for your direction.

And as she learns to listen, may she come to understand
that because you live in and through her,
your still, small voice is also the voice of her deepest inner
knowing.

May she learn to love the sound of her true self.
May she learn that it's the sound of you.

Amen.

for a faith community

O Goodness Gatherer,

My daughter is spiritually lonely and longs to be companioned
on her journey of faith.
Gather those who can sojourn alongside her.
May they be compassionate, inclusive, sincere, and kind.
Bring her into a spiritual family that honors you not just in word
but also in true deed.

Preserve her from faith communities that are unhealthy, imbal-
anced, or toxic.
Give her a discerning mind to make choices that are good not
just for her spiritual health but for her mental health as well, for
one can't exist without the other.

Bring to my daughter friends who are spiritually curious and
inwardly free.

May she and her community grow in love and justice, prayer and activism.

May they advance the cause of love as they seek you together.

Amen.

for embodied knowing

O Indwelling Presence,

When my daughter raises her chin to find you in the sky, gently lower her gaze,
for you delight to abide not only in heaven but also in her belly.

Reveal yourself to her through
the wind in her hair,
the tension in her shoulders,
the peace of her breath,
the warning in her gut.

May she find the root of her spirituality not in a place she can go but in a Person she can know. And may she understand that her own body is the conduit of that knowing.

Amen.

for seeing women lead in church

O Defender of Marginalized Voices,

How can my daughter believe in equality
if it is not practiced in the place she worships a God of justice?

How can I tell her she can grow to be anything
while knowing her most sacred spaces have glass ceilings over-
head?

How will my daughter have courage to follow your call
if she doesn't see other women doing it too?

Surround her with such women.
Fill our churches and religious spaces with such women.
Put such women in decision-making seats there.
Give such women vote and voice and vocation.

When their knees quake,
when they are infantilized,

when they are refused,
when they are mocked,

let it be my daughter's face they see when they close their eyes,
and may they step into their calling anyway.

Amen.

for curiosity

O Star of Wonder,

Give my daughter the gift of wonder. The gift of a curious soul.
The gift of not needing all the answers.

Spare her the suffocation of closed-mindedness
and the loneliness of arrogance.
May she rejoice in finding that
love is not contingent on certainty,
and faith does not necessitate self-righteousness.
Let my daughter seek to learn
from everyone she meets
and every spirituality she encounters—
even and especially from those that feel least familiar.

May the millions of ways humans reach for you
draw her deeper and deeper under love's outstretched wings.

Amen.

for the heart of a mystic

O Universal Lover,

Reveal yourself so perfectly to my daughter that she may readily and eagerly—heart-longingly—give willing consent to a lifelong love affair with you.

Give her the heart of a mystic.
One who sees the strand of love woven in and through all things.
One who is lovestruck, smitten, hopelessly gone,
who so fiercely feels her own belovedness
that she can't help but respond with love in kind.

May this love
empower her,
humble her,
impassion her,
compel her,
fascinate her,
and embolden her.

I pray that she would be so inebriated with this love that when she looks at the starry night sky or the redwood forest or the man on death row or the infant demanding her every cell,

this love may be all she sees.

Amen.

for an unquenched flame

O Sacred Fire,

Captivate my daughter with the mysteries of your holy flame. Let her taste what it is to live ablaze, ignited by a force powerful enough to consume.

There will be wolves with teeth bared who will seek to snuff out her flame.

Protect her.

There will also be wolves in sheep's clothing—harder to spot— who will not gather their breath to huff and puff, but will slowly suffocate her flame and cause it to dull and flicker low.
They will not reveal themselves, so long as she is pleasant and obedient and doesn't rock the boat.

Protect her.

My daughter's flame will shift and morph—in color and heat
and shape—and one day this may frighten her.
Give her the courage to remain open when this happens.
Teach her that she can stand upright and not burn away.

May her spirit blaze; may her fire go unquenched.

Amen.

for freedom

O Faithful Liberator,

To be human is to seek control over our surroundings, circumstances, and relationships.
Yet freedom can be found only in the release.

Unclench my daughter's fists from holding on too tightly to the desire to control.
Invite her to experience the freedom of letting go.
Liberate her from the burden of expectations:
the expectations of society, of authority figures, of herself,

yes, even my own.

You Who Break Every Chain,
set my daughter free from the lure of worldly success and people pleasing.
May she please herself.
And in so doing, may she please you.

May her trust be radical.
May her assurance be steadfast.
May she not stake her identity in obtaining a certain outcome
but rather know who she is when the curtain falls.

May my daughter be inwardly, blissfully, free.

Amen.

WOMANHOOD

for making room for all

O Trustworthy Abundance,

You are generosity itself.
In you there is no lack.

And yet much fear resides among women:
the fear that there is a shortage of goodness,
that there is somehow not enough to go around.
The fear that successful women,
beautiful women,
talented women,
admired women,
are our competition,
and so positions must be fought for.

Spare my daughter of this deception
in the junior high classroom and in the boardroom.
Spare her from the twisted hope that other girls might have less

so that she can have more.
Spare her from a cutthroat culture
that would pit women against women.

May she be one who lifts other women higher, never hoping
that they fall.
May she believe they will go further together than they will alone.

Amen.

for a world without photoshop

O Creator of Cellulite
(and wrinkles and moles and back rolls and bunions),

The signature intrigue in your artwork can make us uncomfortable.
We want perfection; you want distinction.
We want smoothness; you want exhilaration.
We have morphed our perception of beauty into something un-
recognizable to you.

I want so much more for my daughter.

So I pray you would give her eyes to behold her own beauty:
a beauty that is unique,
true,
natural,
all her own;
a beauty that
mimics a rushing river or thunderous sky;

a beauty that isn't meant to hang in a frame but finds its life out in the world.

And, O Most Brilliant Artist,
do not stop with my daughter but give such sight to all of us
so that we can restore this society that wants to erase experience
and conform characters,
so that we can collectively heal
and collectively grieve
and collectively take back what has been lost.

For the sake of all our daughters.

Amen.

for renewed language about womanhood

O Breath Who Spoke the World into Existence,

Give us fresh imagination for the experience of being female.
Give us liberated constructs.
Give us renewed language.
Give us wilder hopes.

I pray my daughter would reject language that tries to limit the possibilities before her and within her. I pray for less "either/or" and for more "both/and."

Keep the word "should" away from my daughter's lips. Let her throat practice the word "desire" instead.

May she speak less of obligations and more of passions. May she hold in reverence the power of the tongue.

Make my daughter aware of the boundaries of language: the way it can limit us. The way it, too, can free us. Help her choose accordingly.

Amen.

for the women who came before

O Ancient of Days,

Every woman who came before my daughter,
every woman who—known or unknown—changed the course
of her life,
each one who deposited something into her soul,
they are all still living and whole in you.

I lift a heart of gratitude to them,
to you,
to a wisdom that could be so brilliant
as to imagine woman in the first place.

Thank you for the women who came before:
the ones who silently guide my daughter,
the ones who pray for her,

the ones who protect her,
the ones on whose shoulders she stands.

Thank you that we are not alone.

Amen.

for the women who will come after

O Lingering One,

There will come a day when my daughter shall be on this earth no more,
her life a mere memory on a page or on a tongue.
There will be women left behind who have been knowingly formed by her.
There will be many others whom she will have helped form without ever having met them.

I pray for the women who will be touched by the ripples of my daughter's life,
whether by blood or proximity or happenstance.
May they carry on the best of her.
May she live in such a way that the best of her is easy to carry on.

I pray for these women,
these miracle creatures who are to come after my daughter.
I pray that they may be a little bit braver,
a little bit kinder,
a little bit more creative,
a little bit more free
because of her.

Let it be so.

Amen.

for intersectional justice

O Center of the Universe,

In you all things find their being and their meaning. In you all things come together. In you all things take root, and in you all things branch out.

As my daughter works for the liberation of all women, I pray she would have eyes to see the bigger picture. May her vision for women be vast, not narrow; inclusive, not exclusive. May she listen for the voices that have historically been drowned out: the voices of women who are elderly, disabled, neurodivergent, racially marginalized, sexually marginalized, or otherwise pushed out of the conversation on feminism.

My prayer for my daughter is that she will always have an ear inclined to those with the least amount of power, the ones whose stories are not lucrative to tell. Give her the wisdom to acknowledge the intersection of identities. Give her the clarity to understand why it matters that she does. And as my daughter seeks to uplift women, may she always bring the ladder first to those who have historically been forgotten.

Amen.

for a feminine imaging of God

O Face of the Divine Feminine,

My daughter bears the *imago Dei*, the image of God, in her body and femininity. And yet it is rare for her to see that represented in sacred spaces. How can she believe in her own *imago Dei* when it has been stifled and subdued in our collective religious imagination?

And so I pray.

I pray for a great awakening to the divine feminine.
I pray for artists to create from it.
I pray for pastors to preach on it.
I pray for liturgists to include it.
I pray for activists to draw strength from it.
I pray for my daughter to delight in it.

Do a new thing within the hearts of the people of God. Crack us open. Give us freer imaginations. Expand our souls to embrace you in the feminine after so long in the masculine. Parts of us will be healed; parts of us will be challenged. Let us be unafraid to be changed.

And when my daughter walks into a place of worship, let it be with her head held high and certainty in her bones, knowing that the essence of who she is reveals to the world the truth of the sacred feminine.

Amen.

for taking up space

O Expansive One,

For so long women have been told not to take up too much
space:
not with their bodies,
not with their voices,
not with their demands and desires.

Society has assured us that the ideal woman is small:
small in body,
small in voice,
small in demands and desires.

May it never be so for my daughter.
May the very idea make her laugh.
May she know *that she knows that she knows*
that she is worthy of taking up space.

May she give her body permission to be whatever size it needs to be.
May she believe her voice is important to be heard.
May she be certain that her demands are reasonable
and that her desires point her to you.

May my daughter refuse to make her life small. May she always take up space.

Amen.

for vocational choice

O You Who Take a Thousand Shapes,

As my daughter discerns the biggest decisions in her life, may she trust the wisdom within herself that is your Spirit.

Whether she marries or remains single,
has children or does not,
works at home or away from it,
may she feel the dignity of her own autonomy.

May she always believe that her life serves a great purpose, however she spends her days. May she find meaning in the small accomplishments as well as the large ones.

My hope for my daughter is that she would feel confident in her own life choices: not comparing herself to another, not wondering if she chose wisely.

Give her keen vision as she makes vocational choices. May she know herself deeply and make decisions from that place of knowing.

Give me the grace to support her in whatever she decides. May the practice of trusting my daughter help me to trust myself.

Amen.

for honoring mother earth

O Original Fertility,

Your abundant love sources all things.
Your generosity creates life in all its forms.
Your fecundity sustains the world.

Captivate my daughter by the divine feminine within creation.
Awe her with a vision of how you mother through atoms and
matter.
Mystify her with the eternal nature of such a life force.
Take her breath away.

When my daughter doubts your care,
when she struggles to feel your presence,
when uncertainty unnerves her,
may she feel right back at home when she steps outdoors.

Let the animals preach to her.
Let the tree roots prophesy to her.

Let the rocks cry out of all the ways she is held.
Under the canopy of stars, give her a cathedral that will never
let her down.

And in return for being mothered so lavishly
may she care for the earth as though for a matriarch,
with honor, respect, and the deepest commitment of love.

Amen.

WHOLENESS

for trying and failing

O Unshaken One,

It is in falling down that we learn to walk,
in stumbling that we learn to pick ourselves back up.
Grant my daughter the courage to take risks,
the understanding that risk may mean failure,
and the perseverance to try again—having learned from her
mistakes.

When she is two and when she is sixty-two,
release my girl from the fear of failure.
Instead, may she welcome it,
knowing it is only in doing so that she becomes brave,
knowing it is only in doing so that she frees her creativity.

I pray you would spare her
from a life half-lived,
a life devoured by fear.

Give her the courage to try and the self-compassion to fail.
Give her a life that devours fear.

Amen.

for getting her butt into counseling

O Safe Haven,

My daughter's sorrows have bruised her soul, and traumas have blurred her vision,
Life has demanded her strength, and now she doesn't know how to be anything but strong.
She grits her teeth even as her heart breaks.
And yet her pride would have her believe she can find healing without help.

And so, gentle Queen of Heaven, I pray for her to get her butt into counseling.

May she show up for the work when she'd rather stay home.
May she look upon her own shadow and learn to welcome it.
May she care for herself in the ways that nourish her most.
May she re-parent herself in the ways I fell short.

May she realize that the strength that once protected her is no longer required, and that the strongest thing she can do now is embrace her weakness.

Bring her the right counselor, I pray. Make them wise, perceptive, and compassionate. Give them eyes to see my daughter. And through them, give my daughter eyes to see herself.

Amen.

for wisdom

O *Everpresent Sophia,*

Let my daughter know you as such, for that is your name in the ancient Scriptures.
You are feminine, indwelling, and active.
You are always accessible but never forceful.
You have secrets to reveal and secrets to keep.
You are a mystery: a holy, holy mystery.

Grant that my daughter may be a woman of wisdom. May she recognize that wisdom does not come from knowledge memorized or advice taken, but that you, Wisdom, already dwell in the deepest parts of her. All she needs to do is still herself and listen.

As a woman of wisdom, may my daughter introduce many more women to Sophia, who dwells within them too. In leadership roles, may she resist the lure of power and instead teach others how to encounter Sophia in the wildest caves of their own souls.

Grant my daughter wisdom. Not for worldly esteem, but for inner peace and righteousness.

Amen.

for welcoming grief

O Keeper of Tears,

I would do anything to barricade my daughter from sadness
and pain,
but I cannot and have not.
So when the grief rolls in, for the first time or for the hundredth
time,
teach her, somehow, to welcome it.
Because her grief means she cared.
Her grief means she loved.
Her grief means it was real.

And so in honor of what could have been,
in honor of what was lost,
in honor of a story that might have ended differently,
may she not run from her grief.
Instead, let her sit with it like a friend,
like a teacher,

like an unexpected comforter.
And in staying present to her grief on the days when it comes
around,
may she be able to live a fuller life on the days when it doesn't.

May she feel it all.
May she hold it all.
May she welcome it all.
Because everything belongs.

Amen.

for befriending anger

O Rolling Thunder,

Women are wary of their anger.
Anger can feel threatening. Wild. Unpredictable.

Women are afraid that if they open Pandora's box, they will never
stop raging.
The hurt has been too deep.
The injustices have been too many.
The fury has been domesticated.
If women let it out, they might never recover.

But perhaps it is not about recovering but uncovering.

Uncover my daughter's anger, O Rolling Thunder. Let silent
repression never be her fate. Let her feel her anger; let her taste
it. Let her listen to her anger, because it tells her the truth. Her
anger tells her what is wrong, what is not as it should be, what
is not as you intended.

She can trust her anger.

After she has felt it, for as long as she needs to feel it, make it clear to her what to do with it. Show her how to channel her anger into change, into action. Show her how to leverage her power to make things right.

Amen.

for the creative life

O Generative One,

Your fruitfulness is alive and well in my daughter's soul. When I listen to her ideas, witness her projects, or behold her vision, I am reminded of you. Within her is the same Spirit that breathed the world into being.

But living a creative life brings vulnerability, and the path is full of highs and lows. Created in your image, my daughter is a creator. But living as such comes with a cost. And so I pray:

When she is a ball of restless energy, give her focus.

When her vision is ahead of her skill, give her dedication.

When she is certain her work is garbage, give her perspective.

When she fears rejection, give her courage.

When she is anxious to see her vision come to life, give her patience.

When her best idea flops, give her a better one.

When she receives a harsh critique, give her teachability.

Above all, may she concern herself less with creative success and more with a fruitful life. May she live out her creativity in ways both seen and unseen by the public eye—with nothing to prove but everything to give.

For we need everything she has to give.

Amen.

for telling the truth

O You Whose Truth Sets Us Free,

Put the truth in my daughter's throat and on her lips.

May she tell the truth when she fears punishment.

May she tell the truth when it will cause discomfort for others.

May she tell the truth when it carries consequences.

May she tell the truth when it will cost her friends.

May she tell the truth when it benefits her enemies.

May she tell the truth when it speaks against power.

May she tell the truth when it will heal others.

May she tell the truth when it will heal her.

May she tell the truth when it makes her seem weak.

May she tell the truth when courage is required.

May she tell the truth, and may the truth always set her free.

Amen.

for healthy boundaries

O Fortress of Loving-Kindness,

The world will try to convince my daughter
that she owes it her time,
her energy,
her emotional availability,
her work.
Left unchecked, the world will consume her
until she exists only for the whims of others.

May it never be so.

Teach her when to say no.
Teach her when to draw a line.
Teach her when to give of herself and when to choose herself.

For it is only through boundaries that she can be protected from
resentment.

It is only through boundaries that she can retain her compassion. And it is only through boundaries that she can care for herself as one worthy
of time,
energy,
emotional availability,
and work.

May my daughter protect herself with the boundaries she needs to live an authentically generous life.

Amen.

for times of depression

O Passionate Blaze,

When the flame of my daughter's desire has blown out,
when her days feel dreary and listless,
when she is unsure of her purpose or direction,
come in a blaze of glory
or in a small, flickering spark,
and light the way back to the fire within.

Give her tools for self-knowledge,
reliable means of getting back in touch with her heart's desires.
Show her practices of prayer
and ways of being
that can breathe life into the weariness of her soul.
Remind her how to find her way back to herself.

When depression sets in, teach her not to panic
but to trust she can find you

in the cloud of unknowing.
For your presence never lifts
but stays ever near.
May she feel you beside her, today and always.

Amen.

for making decisions

O You, Our Start and Destination,

My daughter has come to a crossroads.
Teach her to wait. She has more time than she thinks.

Give her the patience of unhurried discernment
and the trust that you will show her the way.

Alleviate the pressure she feels;
assure her that all shall be well.

As she prays, waits, considers, thinks,
teach her what it means to be inwardly still.

Teach her your ways of deep listening.
May she trust the knowing of her bones.

In this and all decisions, may she consider the good
of others as well as herself.

But above all, may she never worry
about choosing something that is not your will.

Because the very act of listening
means she will not be separated from you.

Amen.

JUSTICE

for raising her voice

O Loving Songstress,

Since the day she was born my daughter has raised her voice, a squawking newborn who believed she was worth our time.

But as she grows older, she will wonder if there is a place setting for her at the table of the world. She will notice that the girls who relinquish their voices are rewarded by the powers that be and that those who refuse to be silent get labeled and hushed and jeered.

And there will come a day when she must decide whether she will speak.

When she opens her mouth, make it her voice that pours forth, not the echo of another's. Give her humility and love, yes, but also give her a firm resolve and loyalty to the light within her.

May she never stop believing that her voice is still worth our time.

Amen.

for leveraging her privilege

O Great Equalizer,

Our family has been given much, so we know that much will be required of us. As my daughter grows observant and thoughtful, asking hard questions, grant her the wisdom to assess how she can best serve her neighbor—and what personal sacrifices it might require to do so.

In the ways that my daughter enjoys social privilege (whether it comes in the form of race, sexuality, thinness, conventional beauty, wealth, etc.), show her those at whose expense such privilege comes. Open her eyes to the suffering of those not like her. Open her eyes to the sins of a society that treats equal human beings so very unequally.

Give my daughter compassion and empathy.
Give her zeal for justice and equity.

But above all, You Who Level All Playing Fields, make it personal: let her be willing to give up her own privilege in order for others to have more dignified lives.

Amen.

for making a home of welcome

O You, Our Home beyond Time and Space,

Take my daughter's hand as she builds a place of her own. May it be the deepest reflection of who she is: through the art on walls, the books on shelves, the pictures in frames, the plants in pots.

But most of all, through the people to whom she opens its doors.

Here in this home may the lonely be embraced, may the grieving be comforted, may the hungry be fed, and may the rejoicing find someone to share in their celebration.

I pray that in this home she is making, living will take precedence over staging. That beauty will be sought and welcomed but so too will the messes. That at the end of the day, whatever condition the baseboards and bathroom sinks may be in, every person who lays their head down here will have no doubt they are loved.

And as one by one people join my daughter's family, whether forever or for a little while, I pray the rooms will expand to contain every drop of love within you, until it goes inching toward the windowsills and leaking out the doorways, streaming down the streets as if they were made of gold.

Amen.

for nonviolence

O Violence Ender,

You who broker peace, disrupt the cycles of violence that live in my daughter's body. For they are sneaky. Subtle. With devilish claws that hook in hidden places:

violence of the tongue,
violence of the heart,
violence of the eye,
violence of the body.

My daughter seeks no harm, and yet it is she who suffers first. End the violence against herself. Teach her to spot it, to name it, to refuse it.

Teach her to speak peace to the storm. Make her like Stella Maris, Our Lady of the Sea, who calms the raging waters of humanity. Teach my daughter the language that stills the deadly waves.

Give her an authentic spirit of pacifism, one that softens not only her fists but also her mind.

My daughter, the peacemaker.
My daughter, the cycle-breaker.
My daughter, the way-paver.

May her softness be her strength.

Amen.

for the common good

O All in All,

Give my daughter a panoramic view of the world. Let her see the whole rather than the parts. May she sense the urgency of your call to care for others and set it as a spiritual practice.

So that when she raises her voice,
casts her vote,
holds her protest sign,
spends her money,
devotes her time,
selects her books,
she will be doing all of these in pursuit of the common good. She will be doing all of these knowing that her neighbor is a part of herself.

Transform her own personal pain into passion for the pain of the world. May her soul only expand, never shrink, from its own grief and loss. For all the ways her heart has been and is still yet to be broken, may she find in piecing it back together that it takes on the shape of the world. And in that shape may she find her fullest self.

Amen.

for small activism

O You Who Plant Trees from Mustard Seeds,

When my daughter becomes despairing over the state of the world
—which she will—

when she realizes that her biggest efforts are only a ripple in the pond
—which is true—

when she wants to give up because caring just hurts too much
—which it does—

bring her back to the face right in front of her. Remind her that smallness is not the same as nothingness. Get her to take a nap. Pour her some water.

And when she is ready once more
—which she will be—

present before her actions she can take
in her town,
on her street,
in her home,
in the smallest spaces, the least sexy spaces, the spaces that don't
seem to matter much.

Stroke her hair and whisper in her ear,
Now then, my beloved, this is how you change the world.

Amen.

for doing the inner work

O Kind Conviction,

It is so much easier to attempt to fight injustice around us than to fight injustice within us. But if we are listening, we know that both are necessary.

May my daughter be one who listens.

May she not hide from her own shadow. May she not run from self-examination. May she not seek to uproot the sin in society without having pulled the gnarled splinters out of her own heart first. In her earnestness for a good and true world, may she not bypass the inner work that you are calling forth in her.

Spare my daughter from performative action devoid of honesty. For her soul will know the truth, and, left unheeded, it will rot her from the inside out.

Help me as I walk my own path of confronting racism, sexism, homophobia, transphobia, ableism, classism, ageism, and everything else that keeps me from wholeness in God. May I be vulnerable and brave in facing my own shadow so that my daughter can be vulnerable and brave in facing hers. Set us both free, O Kind Conviction.

Amen.

for loving her enemy

O Divine Breath,

May my daughter see a human when she imagines her enemy's face.

(breath)

May she find compassion for their brokenness.

(breath)

May she erect the boundaries necessary for her own safekeeping.

(breath)

May she release what is not hers to carry.

(breath)

Amen.

for protecting the vulnerable

O Defending Mother,

You gather the vulnerable like chicks under your wings. You roar out your protection, pushing your cubs behind your back. Teach my daughter the ancient ways of a mothering God: the embodied ways, the earthen ways. Show her where the bones of advocacy reside in her body. May she always leave the ninety-nine in search of the one.

Give my daughter vision for a society that liberates the marginalized rather than takes advantage of them. May she ever and always work toward liberation. May she be willing to give up her own rights to see it come to pass. Awake within my daughter the feminine wisdom that knows we will never be whole until the smallest among us are whole.

May she have the eyes of a prophetess.

Amen.

for breaking bread with others

O Setter of the Cosmic Table,

You line up mercy beside loving-kindness:
a cup of blessing here, a bowl of forgiveness there.
You welcome all to your table,
pulling up extra chairs as more arrive.
At your table, there is no such thing as full.
There is no such thing as "no room."
There is no such thing as scarcity.

You serve your own flesh as the main course,
bread of life to nourish our famished souls.
We feast upon your essence.

At your table are many unknown to my daughter—
those who seem scary,
strange,
unknowable.
Other.

As they linger at your table, as their elbows brush hers,
may my daughter begin to see similarity
where once there was only difference.

There is enough for all, you gleefully declare.
Enough room.
Enough love.
Enough mercy.
There is enough. There is always enough.

And so I pray my daughter hears and understands.

Amen.

EQUALITY

for equal pay

O You Who See All,

You see my daughter.
You see her labor. Her commitment. Her passion.
You see her skill. Her ability. Her expertise.

You see her paycheck. And you see the paychecks of her male colleagues.

Equalize them, I pray.

May my daughter receive fair wages for her hard work.
May *every* daughter receive fair wages for her hard work.
May we reject the passive acceptance of "a man's world"
and instead demand that justice be served.
May we, collectively, settle for nothing less.

The world we are passing on to our daughters still bends toward our sons.

All these years, and still the wage gap persists.
Nevertheless, may she persist.
May we persist.
May justice persist.

Amen.

for promotions and leadership positions

O Lifter of the Marginalized,

It is said that you cast down the mighty from their thrones and lift up the lowly. As unfair as it is, my daughter is one of the lowly in her profession: a female in an environment that systematically rewards males. Like so many women before her, her work has been undervalued and overlooked. Others have risen through the ranks while she has been met with a pat on the head.

And so I pray: open doors for her.

May she be promoted. May she be given a raise. May she receive unexpected job offers and unlikely opportunities. May she be placed in leadership positions where everyone can watch her shine. May opportunity rain down on her.

May she, for once, be relieved of the fatigue that women feel when passed by for less-qualified men.

Amen.

for felt safety

O Haven of Safekeeping,

Is it too much to ask for my daughter to feel safe when she walks to her car at night?

Is it too much to ask for my daughter not to fear when politely turning down a stranger?

Is it too much to ask for my daughter to think only of what brings her joy when getting dressed?

Is it too much to ask for my daughter not to need to have a plan ready in case of assault?

Is it too much to ask for my daughter to feel as safe as my sons?

Is it too much to ask of you? Of a society? Of men?

Because it feels like too much to ask of her.

May my daughter not be a prisoner of fear.
May I not be a prisoner of anger.
May you hold us both in the palm of your soft, safe hand.

Amen.

for when she is mansplained

O Word of Wisdom,

You have given my daughter a voice. You have given her wisdom—
sophia—and she knows well of that which she speaks.

When she is treated as inferior because of her gender, embolden
her.

When she is spoken down to, equip her.

When she is infantilized, lift her chin.

O *Logos* of the ages, open her mouth to communicate that which
you have revealed to her, whether it be theology or politics or
science or animal husbandry or nail art or basket weaving.

May she know that whatever knowledge she has labored for, it
is real and deserving of dignity.

May your presence give her the confidence to stand her ground and hold their gaze.

May she be unable to be cut down.

Let my daughter grow ever more in knowledge, wisdom, and expertise. Because the world needs her brilliant mind.

Amen.

for a just maternity leave

O Eternal Doula,

You care tenderly for the body and soul of my daughter,
advocating for an experience in the world that is fair and true,
consoling her in your embrace when it fails to be so.
As she serves all of humankind by bringing a child into the world,
I pray:
make her maternity leave long and make it just.

May she be fairly compensated by her employer
for the hours of labor and delivery,
for the sleepless nights,
and thankless days,
for the time to heal her body
and tend to her mind.

I pray that my daughter's boss would honor her,
that her coworkers would support her,

and that she would not be pressured into returning to work before she is ready.
May time be a gift, as she takes all that she needs.

And for every mother around the world who is given no consideration
for her indispensable role in the continuation of life,
I pray for heavenly consolation
and earthly change.

May it be so.

Amen.

for representation

O Universal Mirror,

You reflect back to us our truest selves,
and we cannot know ourselves apart from gazing at you.
In your mirror, may my daughter see her face.

And because imagination depends on perception,
may my daughter perceive herself, too, in the women she admires.
May they share her skin color. Her hair texture. Her field of
passion.
May they share her personality traits. Her disabilities. Her socio-
economic class.
May they share her marginalization. Her determination. The
sparkle in her eyes.

May they share the parts of her that she questions,
the parts of her that make her feel most isolated and alone.
Give her women to look to.

Give her an imagination for what could be.
Give her the hope of a future yet unseen.

Give my daughter role models who are worthy of her.

Amen.

for support in the face of sexual harrassment

O Feminine Defender,

My daughter's body is an image of the divine. Her mind was created to be a safe and peaceful space of refuge. I pray, hold her body and her mind under the mantle of your fierce guardianship.

Protect my daughter from being victimized by sexual harassment. Protect her from men on the street or in the workplace or in the classroom or in the church pews who would have the audacity to violate the holiness of her body and mind.

Empower her to give harassment a name—to call it what it is, both to her perpetrator and to those in the larger system. When she is disbelieved or mocked, make her sure and courageous. Give her the strength to advocate for the truth and for the dignity of all women.

Incline those around her to believe her. Support her. Side with her. Seek justice with her. Gather your forces, male and female, who will raise their voices alongside my daughter's voice. Give her the gift that so many women have been denied: the gift of being believed.

Amen.

for marriage partnership

O Source of Our Balance,

In you there is no male or female,
only being.
Under your cosmic roof there is no sexism or misogyny,
only equality.
From under the shadow of your wing,
both women and men emerge in total freedom.

And so, I pray, may it be in my daughter's home,
on earth as it is in heaven.

May her marriage be a true partnership.
May household labor and the care of children be shared.
May the voices of all be heeded.
May theirs be a home of community and receptivity.

I pray that my daughter would know the joy of a marriage between equals.
I pray she would not settle for anything less.

Amen.

for women's ordination

O Truest Bread and Wine,

You nourish us as a mother does,
feeding us from your very body,
saying, "Take and eat."

You are the giver and sustainer of life,
the one who calls and the one to whom we each must answer.

You pour out your Spirit on your sons and your daughters.
So I pray:
if you call my daughter to be a priest or pastor,
let no man stand in her way.
Make a path for her to answer your call.
Give her the strength and stamina to follow your voice.

And if she one day ministers to your beloved people,
may they be nourished as by a mother

who feeds them as though from her very body, saying, "Take and eat."

Amen.

for the global sisterhood

O Thread of Solidarity,

You weave your way through one woman and the next, connecting in spirit those who live worlds apart. As my daughter faces the very real challenges of womanhood in her Western context, may she also carry the burdens of her sisters around the globe:

for the daughters who are abandoned in favor of sons,
for the daughters who are denied an education,
for the daughters who do not have the right to vote,
for the daughters who are refused a driver's license,
for the daughters who are victims of genital mutilation,
for the daughters who are given in marriage as mere children,
for the daughters who routinely suffer abuse.

For these and others whose pain is more acute than her own,
may she feel empathy.
May she draw strength.

May she support change.
May she be compelled to pray.
May she carry her sisters.

May my daughter's world always be bigger than her own singular experience of it.

Amen.

MILESTONES

for learning to walk

O Courageous One,

My daughter is taking her first steps.
I stand behind her, cheering her on.
She is learning to walk, and I am learning to let go.

May the world open up its magic before her,
inviting her to explore,
inviting her to bravery
and curiosity
and adventure.

Let me not caution her, as society is wont to do with our little
girls, but encourage her strength and mastery. Let her hear
me say "You can do it!" far more than she hears me say "Be
careful!"

May my daughter celebrate her accomplishment and marvel at her body. May I never forget the look on her face as she does. And may I see it a thousand more times in the years to come.

Amen.

for starting kindergarten

O Divine Releaser,

With grace and tenderness you let your children go. You are always near, always ready, but still you offer our release. Freedom, you say, requires it.

I confess I struggle, O my Heavenly Parent. I grieve the loss of control over my daughter's life even while celebrating and enjoying her independence. Help me trust the process, knowing I can mourn what is behind while welcoming what is before.

Guide my daughter in the path of inner freedom. Even as I practice releasing her from my own grip, teach her how to release herself from the grip of conformity, comparison, and people pleasing. Give her the strength to be exactly who she is: free and released and beloved.

When she leaves my arms and walks into that classroom, may she begin the journey of knowing what it is to be inwardly alone with you.

Amen.

for menarche (first menstruation)

O Great Life-Spiller,

In your wisdom you created the female body to mirror your divine nature: growth, fruit, death, new beginnings—over and over again. The cycle of life-death-resurrection is borne witness to through my daughter's flowering reproductive system.

On this, her first blood, I lift my daughter to the moon she mirrors in filling and in emptying, and I honor her womanhood. I stand with the women elders of the ages and invite her into the circle of knowing.

Bless her, you whose blood has given life to all things. May my daughter know what it is to be held by you. In her blood and in her discomfort, may she see the dignity of carrying your sacred mantle.

She, a harbinger of life and death.

She, a prophetic sign to a world not given to believe in resurrection.

She, a promise, a symbol; her blood its own kind of eucharist.

Amen.

for leaving home

O God Ever Near,

As my daughter embarks out into the world without me, I pray that you would enhance her wisdom and discernment. Make her sharp and perceptive, able to protect herself with clear decisions and shrewd choices.

But I know that part of growing up requires youthful foolishness. Mistakes will be made and consequences suffered. When this happens, make me as merciful and compassionate a parent as you are. Help me to listen before I scold, to consider before I jump to conclusions.

As she learns to become an adult and to make her way through the adult world, I pray not that she may avoid suffering but simply that she may suffer only what she can bear. O Sacred Companion, protect my daughter from that which is too much for her heart. Do not depart from her, but stay near and present as she finds her way.

If I cannot be at my daughter's side for her whole life (and I know that I cannot), it brings me comfort to know that the same Companion who has never left me will be guiding her too.

Amen.

for her wedding day

O You Who Are Our Wedding Feast,

On this, my daughter's sacred day, lift the burden of details from her shoulders.
Replace it with a mantle of singing and a garland of joy.

As she embarks on a path she does not yet know, may she rise to the occasion—
grinning in the face of a future that will assuredly hold both pleasure and pain.
May love steady her when she peers shakily into uncertainty.

I pray her marriage may be a promise of mutual self-giving.
I pray that the spouse she has chosen will listen to her ideas, amplify her voice, and encourage her dreams.
May this new family formed today be founded on tender commitment and care.

Long after the glamour of the wedding day passes, may quiet friendship linger on.

Most of all, O Banqueting Table,
today may my daughter feast on the fullness of your presence within her.
May she not enter into marriage seeking to be completed
but because she has already found herself to be complete.

Amen.

for childbirth

O Holy Midwife,

My daughter's rite of passage has come.

Anchor her to the truest parts of herself. Anchor her to you.

She will bear more than she believes she can handle. She will endure more than she thinks she can survive. But she is stronger than she knows, and she is about to find this out.

Let all the saints and angels pray for my baby and for her baby.
Let all the ancestors gather round and hold up my daughter's arms.
Let the moon hang low to watch the magic unfold.
Let critters in the grass outside shush themselves to listen.

A new human person is here to tell us about forever.
A new creature is here to tell us about the Creator.

A new mystery is here to tell us to marvel.
A new hope is here to tell us to never give up.

We bless you, O Great Birther, for this gift of life.

Amen.

for her fortieth birthday

O Life Source,

When I look at my daughter on her fortieth birthday, I celebrate the woman before me. She continues to choose growth. She continues to accept new challenges. She continues to let love expand within her. I am so proud.

In this new chapter of her life, I pray that what is left of my daughter's inhibitions will fall away. I pray that she would feel herself becoming braver by the day, knowing she is no longer that young girl who found her worth in the approval of others. May she move forward as a woman comfortable in her own skin.

I pray that middle age would invite her to fearlessness, to risk-taking, and to self-determining choices. May it also teach her the value of vulnerability, tenderness, and deep listening.

As my daughter embarks on the second half of life, may it be a path of sacred wisdom that is laid out before her.

In the past, people called this birthday "over the hill." But no, not my daughter. My daughter is still fiercely climbing toward the top of the mountain.

Amen.

for menopause

O Tree of Life,

The menstrual cycle roots a woman to the cycles of nature when she is young and needs reminding. But my daughter can now be trusted to remember her rootedness all on her own. She knows who she is, and she knows how to return to the Tree of Life, again and again, as a beloved creature. Bless her.

As her fecundity wanes, I pray that you reveal to her the many ways she bears fruit separate from her reproductive system. Let her see her fertility as boundless, boundary-less. Give her eyes that can recognize her own generativity. Bless her.

As my daughter's sacred blood runs dry, she enters into the fellowship of the elders. No longer a young woman, she now bears the distinction of one with the benefit of wisdom and life experience. She is becoming a part of the foundation: one who holds other females on her shoulders. Bless her.

Amen.

for times of tragedy

O Singular Candle,

In this, my daughter's darkest night, flicker.

In her rage and in her grief, be steady.

In the coldness of the world, give warmth.

When despair knocks on her door, stay near.

As my daughter's world falls apart, as she wonders how anything could ever be alright again, as she struggles to imagine how to move forward, light her way, I pray.

When she isn't sure she can keep going, give her the strength to reach out for the light. Give her the will to take one more step toward it. Give her the hope that the darkness will not overtake her, because you, O Singular Candle, will never burn out.

Amen.

for her death

O Great Mother,

This is the prayer that should never be uttered. No one should outlive their daughter.

And yet . . .

Thank you for her.
Thank you for the electricity of her smile.
Thank you for the sound of her laughter.
Thank you for her gifts and her wisdom and her love.
I even give thanks for the times we fought,
for now I count these times as a privilege;
and for all the gray hairs she gave me,
for I would give anything to witness her troublemaking again.

Her love has changed me.
Loving her has changed me.

In this life and in the next, may she find peace.

May she know what it is to be held by the Great Mother who wipes away every tear from her eye and whispers, "Behold, I make all things new."

Amen.

ACKNOWLEDGMENTS

This book would likely not exist had I not encountered Joyce Rupp's *Fragments of Your Ancient Name* at a point when I desperately needed a renewed imagination for God. For that and for *Prayers to Sophia*, I honor and thank you, Joyce.

Thank you to the team at Brazos Press for bringing this book to life. Because of your professionalism and personalism, I count myself lucky to be in the Brazos family. Thank you also to my agent, Keely Boeving, at WordServe Literary. Working with you is a joy.

My faith has been buoyed through the commitment of my colleagues at the National Catholic Reporter and Global Sisters Report to amplify the voices of women and marginalized people within the Catholic Church. Thank you for your example.

I am grateful for the unfailing love I have in my extended family, especially my dad and mom, Randall and Kay, whose feminist parenting produced this rather spicy daughter.

Eric, your support sustains me. Alyosha, Moses, Taavi, Oscar, and Thea, your way of seeing the world nourishes me. I am the luckiest.

A special thank you to those around the world who are working on behalf of girls and women in so many ways. May you experience the nearness of divine arms holding you as you labor.

And to our Mother/Father/Sister/Brother/Lover/Midwife who art in heaven/on earth/under the earth/in the seas: thank you, most of all, for being love itself.

Shannon K. Evans, a writer in the contemplative Catholic tradition, is the author of *Rewilding Motherhood: Your Path to an Empowered Feminine Spirituality*, *Embracing Weakness: The Unlikely Secret to Changing the World*, and *Luminous: A 30-Day Journal for Accepting Your Body, Honoring Your Soul, and Finding Your Joy*. She is an editor for *National Catholic Reporter*, a writer and retreat leader for the Jesuit Conference of Canada and the United States, and a regular contributor to Franciscan Media. She has written for *U.S. Catholic*, *America*, and *Geez* magazines. Evans speaks regularly at churches, conferences, and retreats on topics related to motherhood, prayer, and justice, and she leads groups in guided meditation. She and her husband are raising five children, five chickens, and one dog on the Iowa prairie.